Contents

Any words appearing in the main text in bold, **like this**, are explained in the Glossary.

At the seashore

Imagine you have been out to sea in a sailing boat, and now you are heading for shore. You are very close to land, so you jump into the shallow, salty water, which reaches up to your waist.

Sights and sounds

As you wade ashore, you hear the waves breaking around you. There are stones beneath your feet. You can feel clumps of seaweed and patches of smooth sand. Ahead there is a sandy beach, and nearby there are rocks and steep cliffs.

This typical seashore has cliffs, rocks and sand.

 habitat explorer

Seashore Explorer

Neil Morris

Raintree

www.raintreepublishers.co.uk

Visit our website to find out more information about **Raintree** books.

To order:

 Phone 44 (0) 1865 888112

 Send a fax to 44 (0) 1865 314091

Visit the Raintree Bookshop at **www.raintreepublishers.co.uk** to browse our catalogue and order online.

First published in Great Britain by Raintree, Halley Court, Jordan Hill, Oxford OX2 8EJ, part of Harcourt Education.
Raintree is a registered trademark of Harcourt Education Ltd.

Editorial: Nick Hunter and Diyan Leake
Design: Michelle Lisseter
Illustration: Bridge Design
Picture Research: Maria Joannou
Production: Jonathan Smith

Originated by Repro Multi Warna
Printed in China by WKT Company Limited

ISBN 1 844 43458 3 (hardback)
08 07 06 05 04
10 9 8 7 6 5 4 3 2 1

ISBN 1 844 43469 9 (paperback)
09 08 07 06 05
10 9 8 7 6 5 4 3 2 1

British Library Cataloguing in Publication Data
Morris, Neil
Seashore Explorer
577.6'99
A full catalogue record for this book is available from the British Library.

Acknowledgements
The publishers would like to thank the following for permission to reproduce photographs: Alamy Images pp. **4**, **16**; Ardea pp. **15** (Liz & Tony Bomford), **22** (John Mason), **24**; Bruce Coleman Collection pp. **26** (Roine Magnusson), **29** (Allan G. Potts); Corbis p. **21**; FLPA pp. **6** (Panda/B. Cranston), **7** (Hugh Clark), **11** (D. P. Wilson), **19** (Ian Rose), **20** (D. P. Wilson); Nature Picture Library pp. **13** (Thomas Lazar), **14** (Sinclair Stammers), **17**, **18**, **25** (William Osborn), **27** (Pete Oxford); NHPA pp. **10** (G. J. Cambridge), **12** (Norbert Wu), **28**; Oxford Scientific Films pp. **8** (Ian West), **9**

Cover photograph of a common hermit crab reproduced with permission of FLPA (Foto Natura Stock/J. Van Arkel)

The publishers would like to thank Louise Spilsbury for her assistance in the preparation of this book.

Every effort has been made to contact copyright holders of any material reproduced in this book. Any omissions will be rectified in subsequent printings if notice is given to the publishers.

The paper used to print this book comes from sustainable resources.

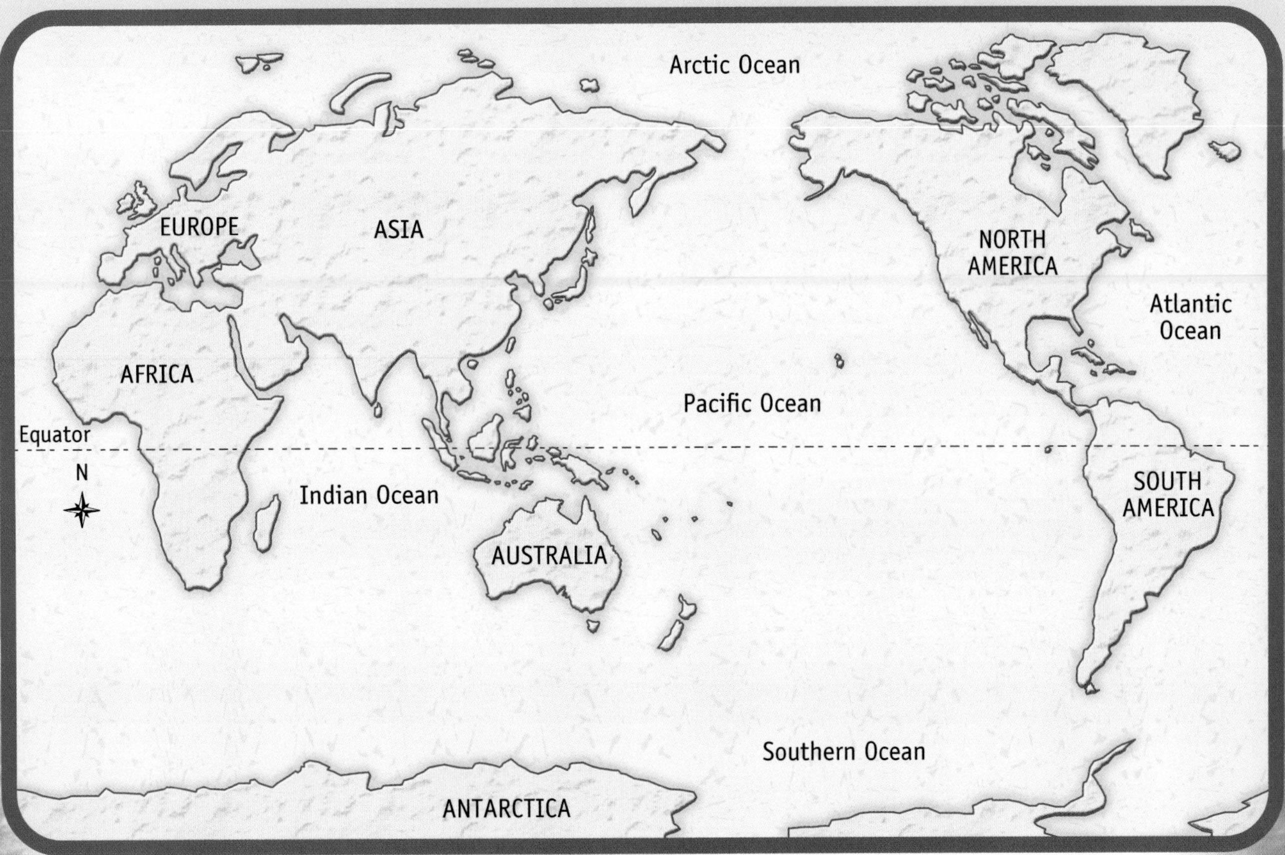
Arctic Ocean
EUROPE
ASIA
NORTH AMERICA
Atlantic Ocean
AFRICA
Pacific Ocean
Equator
N
Indian Ocean
SOUTH AMERICA
AUSTRALIA
Southern Ocean
ANTARCTICA

Seashore habitat

You are going to explore many different parts of the seashore, from sand **dunes** to rock pools. The seashore forms a natural **habitat** or home for many plants and animals, which have specially **adapted** to life in these conditions.

This map shows the world's large land masses, called continents. They are surrounded by oceans. Where land and ocean meet, there is seashore.

Explorer's notes

Land meets sea at the seashore. The seashore is a habitat for plants and animals. The sea is salty, the beach is sandy, and the cliffs are rocky and steep.

In the shallows

Some of the seaweed you see in the shallow water is kelp. This brown plant lives under water but can stay alive on the shore. It needs sunlight to survive, so it grows well in shallow, clear water. Kelp often forms large groups, called kelp forests.

Seaweeds belong to a group of plants called **algae**. There are seaweeds all over the world, but kelps live only in cold waters.

You can see why this kelp is called a forest.

Seaweeds anchor themselves to rocks so they do not get washed away.

Life in the kelp forest

You can see other colours moving among the brown kelp. These are sea animals that have **adapted** to life in the underwater forest. Limpets and sea urchins **graze** on the kelp. Other creatures, such as starfish and small fishes called wrasse, hide among the seaweeds. They are **predators**, on the lookout for shellfish to eat.

Explorer's notes

Predators hunt, catch and kill other animals for food. Starfish are predators. Mussels are the starfishes' **prey**.

At low tide

When the **tide** is out, land is uncovered at the seashore. When the tide is in, more of the shore is covered by water. This region is called the intertidal zone (meaning 'zone between the tides'). Coming out of the sea at low tide, you can stand on the rocky lower shore. As you walk away from the sea, you cross the middle shore, the upper shore, and finally the splash zone.

The rocky lower shore is uncovered at low tide.

Life on the lower shore

The lower shore is only out of the water for a short time, so you will have to explore quickly. You may see some flat periwinkles. Their name is confusing, because the shells of these small sea snails are actually round. You may find periwinkles with green, yellow, orange or black shells. They are about the same size as the bubbles (called bladders) on bladder wrack, a type of seaweed. The periwinkles feed on the wrack and hide beneath it at low tide.

The ins and outs of tides

Twice a day the ocean rises, and seawater covers more land. At high tide, we say that the tide is in. Then it slowly goes out, and the land is uncovered again at low tide.

Flat periwinkles are feeding on bladder wrack here.

On the middle shore

Most of the creatures that you find on the middle shore are protected by hard shells. Mussels crowd together and are easy to find. They attach themselves to rocks with tiny threads. If you try to pull one off (don't try too hard!), you will see how strong they are. Their smooth, black shells are firmly closed. But when the **tide** comes in and covers them, the shells will open so that the mussels can filter seawater for food.

These mussels are crowded together, waiting for the tide to come in.

Sea anemones

Under water, sea anemones look like flowers. But really they are hollow, jellylike animals. When the tide is out, they look like blobs of jelly stuck to a rock. They close up, like mussels, but inside they have lots of **tentacles**. In the water, anemones use these to sting and **paralyse** their **prey**.

Many sea animals have **adapted** the way they live to helping each other. The tiny female pea crab, for example, crawls inside a mussel's shell and lives there. She feeds on the food that the mussel collects, and helps keep the mussel clean.

Explorer's notes

Some seashore rules:
- Disturb animals and plants as little as possible.
- After picking up a rock, replace it gently in the same spot.
- Collect only empty shells, and not too many.

Cone-shaped limpets and closed sea anemones stick firmly to rocks when the tide is out.

On the upper shore

When you explore the rocky upper shore, you will find lots more shelled creatures stuck to the rocks. Some are winkles, such as the rough periwinkle, whose ribbed shell feels bumpy to the touch. Others are barnacles, with their cone-shaped shells. These two-shelled creatures belong to different groups. Winkles are **molluscs**, like oysters and octopuses. Barnacles are **crustaceans**, like crabs and prawns.

These gooseneck barnacles are using their feathery limbs to feed.

Cockle catchers

If you look through binoculars, you may see a small group of oystercatchers on a sandy part of the shore. Their beaks are perfectly shaped for their job – opening cockles and other molluscs (but rarely oysters). The oystercatcher stabs between the two halves of the shellfish or, if it is closed tight, it smashes the shell open. Some molluscs, such as razorshells, escape danger by burrowing down into the sand.

Beachcombers find different shells on beaches washed by warmer, **tropical** waters. One of the largest is the spiral shell of the conch, a kind of sea snail. For thousands of years people have used the empty shells as trumpets.

This American oystercatcher is feeding on a conch.

Miniature seas

There are rock pools on the upper shore. These are exciting places to explore, because they are like miniature seas. Some are topped up with water by every **tide**, but others are only reached by the very highest tides. They make a safe home for many small sea animals and plants. If you sit quietly beside a rock pool, you can watch life going on within a mini-**habitat**.

As you clamber around the rock pools, you may see that they are on a large, flat bed of rock. This is called a wave-cut platform, because it is carved and smoothed over many thousands of years by the action of waves.

This is a hermit crab in its borrowed home.

Slugs and crabs

Sea slugs are often coloured orange or red. They are able to feed on sea anemones without getting stung by their **tentacles**. Slugs have no shell, and the hermit crab does not have a complete shell either.

We call it a hermit because it lives in the empty shells of others. When it outgrows that shell, it will leave it and move into a bigger one.

Explorer's notes

Crustaceans seen in the rock pool:
- barnacles
- prawns
- crabs.

The shore crab has its own shell; the hermit crab borrows from a dead sea snail.

Rock-pool fish

Rock pools are a good place to see fish. You may be surprised how many fish there are. They will dart for cover if disturbed, so it is best to lie down on a rock next to the pool. Then you will not be so easily seen. Small fish such as the goby have eyes on top of their head. This helps them see **predators** such as gulls, which often visit rock pools when looking for food.

Rock pools are full of creatures, including sea anemones.

The shanny mainly feeds on small crustaceans.

The small shanny grows up to ten centimetres long. It is usually a greenish-brown colour and difficult to see against rocks and weeds. It can change colour to match its surroundings.

Special adaptations

Some fish have **adapted** to shallow water by being able to cling tightly to rocks. The lumpsucker fish got its name because it has a sucker on its belly to stick to underwater rocks. The female lumpsucker's eggs also stick to rocks.

Explorer's notes

When animals blend in with the surroundings, it is called **camouflage**. Some small rock-pool fish can change colour and so avoid being seen by predators or **prey**.

Mudflats

Mudflats form near the wide mouths of rivers, called estuaries. When the tide is in, salty seawater mixes with the fresh water flowing down in the river. Mudflats are difficult places to walk, and can be dangerous for human explorers, so it is best just to look, using binoculars.

Some plants are able to grow in mud and salty ground, and they help form salt marshes.

Shelducks sieve the mud and water with their bills, looking for small snails and other food.

Changing seasons

Spotted redshanks and curlews have long bills, which help them dig **molluscs** out of the mudflats. In winter, large flocks of **migratory** birds arrive to find food and shelter. Brent geese fly to warmer coasts from their summer breeding grounds in the Arctic.

Sea asters are common on coastal salt marshes.

Salt-marsh plants

Cord grass gives off salt in the same way animals sweat. Salt-marsh plants produce more seeds than others, because only a few survive to become plants. The seeds attract many birds.

Explorer's notes

Migration – a long journey taken by animals, usually when the seasons change. The animals travel to find warmth, food and shelter.

In the splash zone

There is an area of the beach, just above the normal high-water mark, where it is often quite wet. This is because salty spray is thrown up from the sea, especially when there is a strong wind. During a storm, crashing waves may throw sand and pebbles up here. It is a difficult place to live, but colourful **lichens** often grow here in bands.

Whelks have different coloured shells.

Meat-eating sea snail

Dog whelks are small sea snails, up to 3 centimetres long and yellow, brown or grey in colour. They feed on even smaller acorn barnacles (up to 12 millimetres across), as well as larger mussels. Since their **prey** is too strong to prise off the rocks, the whelks use their long tongues like drills to bore a hole into their shell. If you find barnacles with a hole instead of a closed door at the top of the shell, they were probably eaten by dog whelks.

In warmer parts of the world, a **tropical** splash zone might be almost white. That is because the grains of sand are made up of tiny pieces of broken sea shells and coral.

Explorer's notes

The splash zone is at the top of the upper shore, at the back of the beach. Conditions are usually:
- salty
- windy
- wet.

A sandy tropical beach.

On the strandline

The strandline is a narrow zone at the top of the beach. This is where **debris** gets dumped by the highest **tides**. When you get there, you will probably smell rotting seaweed and find flies buzzing all over it. But this is an excellent place for seashore explorers. If you lift up some dead bladder wrack or other seaweed, you'll see hundreds of tiny sandhoppers leaping in all directions.

These strandlines on a pebbly beach show how high the tide has come.

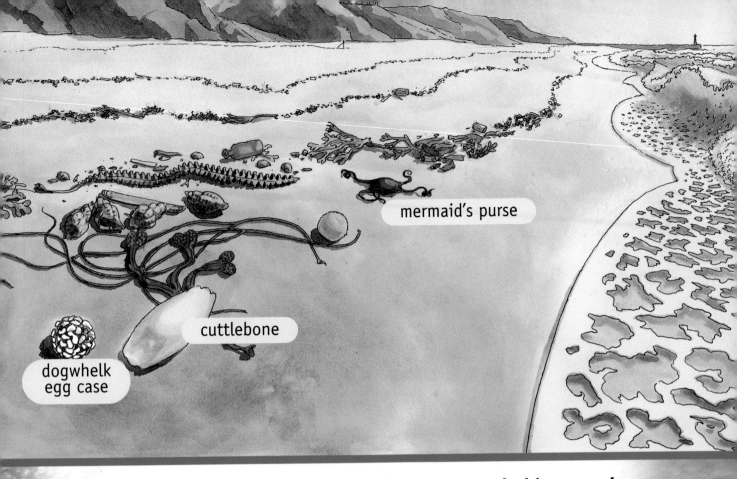

mermaid's purse

cuttlebone

dogwhelk
egg case

**There are natural objects and
debris on the strandline.**

Strange shapes

Beachcombers find all sorts of strange-looking
things on the strandline. There are
usually lots of empty shells, as well as
sea-urchin skeletons and cuttlebones.
The so-called mermaid's purse is the
egg pouch of a dogfish (a small fish
in the shark family). It has curly
tendrils at each corner to help
attach the pouch to seaweed.

Explorer's notes

Finds on the strandline:
- bits of driftwood (some
  rubbed smooth by the sea)
- broken fishing net
- child's plastic spade.
Dangerous items of human
rubbish to avoid:
- broken glass
- lumps of oil
- chemicals.

23

Sand dunes

As you head towards the back of the beach, you can see a group of tall, rounded hills of sand. The sand piled up over time as it was blown towards land by wind off the sea. Then tough plants gained a foothold, and the sand built up around them.

Without the grass, dunes would drift even more in the wind.

This sea holly is growing on a sand dune.

Dune-fixing plants

Sand **dunes** are fixed by plants, and the most
important of these is marram grass. This tough, tall
grass has spreading roots and is happy to have some
of its stems buried in sand. Watch out for another
dune plant, called sea holly. This has sharp spines on
its leaves, putting off any animal that might take a
fancy to it. There are beetles and spiders here, too.
They shelter in tufts of marram grass, and if it is
very hot, they burrow in the sand.

Sand dunes make a good **habitat** for **reptiles**, because they need to
spend time in the sun warming up their cold-blooded bodies. Early
in the morning you might find a sand lizard sunbathing, but it is
well **camouflaged** against the sand. When it has warmed up, the
lizard will go off in search of food.

On the cliffs

Now you are coming to the end of your seashore journey. If you stand at the foot of the cliffs in spring or early summer and look up, you will see thousands of seabirds. Up close the noise is deafening, as the birds' cries echo off the rocks. It is best to use binoculars to bird-watch. You may even spot some nests and eggs. That is why the birds are here. They need somewhere to raise their chicks, and it has to be close to the sea so that they can catch plenty of fish.

Kittiwakes crowd the cliffs above the seashore.

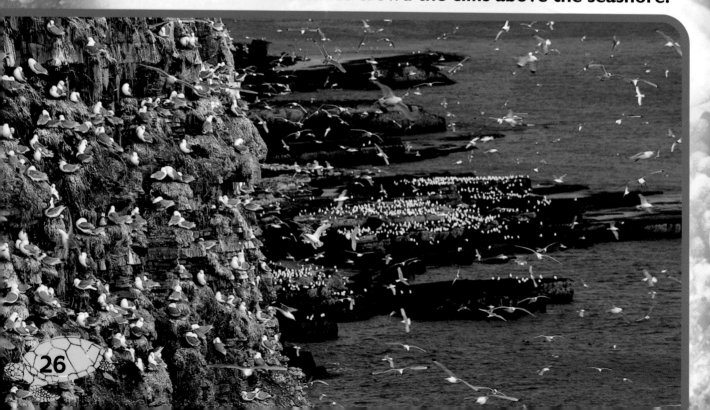

Ledges and burrows

Kittiwakes nest on ledges on the cliff face. These gulls are named after their loud call of *kitti-waak*. They build untidy nests from grass and seaweed that they stick to cracks in the rock with mud. The female kittiwake lays up to three eggs in the nest. **Guillemots** do not bother with a nest. They simply lay their eggs on a cliff ledge.

This puffin has caught plenty of sand eels to feed its chicks.

Explorer's notes

Cliff birds and their nests and eggs:
- kittiwake, seaweeds and mud nest, one to three eggs
- guillemot, no nest, one egg
- puffin, nest in burrow, one egg.

Changing seashores

Seashores change naturally over thousands of years. Conditions change according to the weather, and the way the sea behaves affects the coast. Scientists believe that sea levels are rising around the world. If this carries on, it will change our coastlines.

People change seashores, too. In recent years spills from huge oil tankers have **polluted** coasts around the world, clogging beaches with oil and killing many seabirds and other creatures.

This beach is covered with oil after a spill at sea.

National parks

In many parts of the world, seashores are being turned into national parks. Animals and plants are protected, and people are not allowed to build on or pollute the area. The parks usually include special footpaths, so that visitors can watch birds and look at the scenery without causing any damage.

Explorer's notes

Some explorer's rules:
- Use paths where possible, so as not to wear the ground away
- Leave things exactly as you find them, so as not to harm wildlife
- Never leave rubbish, which would spoil things for others.

Grey seals bask on the seashore.

If we pollute our oceans and coasts, we put wildlife at great risk. That is why it is important to treat the seashore with great respect.

Find out for yourself

You may have the chance to visit the seashore. If you do, look out for different types of **habitats**, and the different types of plants and animals that live there. Perhaps you could compare different shellfish or look at the life in a rockpool.

Using the Internet

Explore the Internet to find out more about the seashore. Websites can change, but if some of the links below no longer work, don't worry. Use a kid-friendly search engine, such as Yahooligans, and type in keywords such as 'beach', 'hermit crab' or the name of a beach near where you live.

Websites

www.mcsuk.org
The Marine Conservation Society is a UK charity working to protect the oceans, coasts and their wildlife.

www.panda.org
WWF (World Wide Fund For Nature) is a global organization that aims to stop the destruction of our natural world.

www.greenpeace.org
Greenpeace is an international non-profit organization working to save the environment.

www.planetark.org
Planet Ark is an Australian non-profit, non-political organization that aims to show people ways to reduce their day-to-day impact on the environment.

Glossary

adapt   change in order to suit the conditions

algae   types of simple plant that grow in water and wet places

beachcomber   someone who collects things that have washed up on the beach

camouflage   blending in with the surroundings, for example by changing colour

crustacean   kind of animal without a backbone and with a hard outer shell, such as a crab, prawn or barnacle

debris   (pronounced DEB-ree) scattered pieces of rubbish

dune   mound or hill of sand

graze   eat plants where they are growing

guillemot   (pronounced GIL-ee-mot) a seabird with a narrow, pointed bill

habitat   natural environment, or home, of an animal or a plant

migratory   a word referring to animals that go on a long journey, usually with the changing seasons

mollusc   animal without a backbone and with a soft body, such as a snail, mussel or octopus

paralyse   cause an animal to lose the ability to move

pollute   damage with harmful substances

predator   animal that hunts and kills other animals for food

prey   animal that is hunted by another animal for food

reptile   animal with a scaly skin, such as a snake, lizard or turtle

tendril   slender, threadlike part

tentacle   long, slender body part used for feeling or grasping

tide   rise and fall of the sea that happens twice a day

tropical   near the hottest region of Earth, the Tropics

Index